THE INFINITE ECONOMY:

HOW WE CAN ALL BE RICH

Vivian Arthur

The Apollo Press
Albuquerque, New Mexico

Man is born free, and everywhere he is in chains.
- Jean Jacques Rousseau (1712-1778)

For every man who lives without freedom, the rest of us must face the guilt.
- Lillian Hellman (1905-1984)

Civilizations, I believe, come to birth and proceed to grow by successfully responding to successive challenges. They break down and go to pieces if and when a challenge confronts them which they fail to meet.
- Arnold Toynbee (1889-1975)

We are all ill: but even a universal sickness implies an idea of health.
- Lionel Trilling (1905-1976)

Mankind always sets itself only such problems as it can solve.
- Karl Marx (1818-1883)

I believe that we are lost here in America, but I believe we shall be found.
- Thomas Wolfe (1900-1938)

These are times in which a genius would wish to live. It is not in the still calm of life, or the repose of a pacific station, that great characters are formed...Great necessities call out great virtues.
- Abigail Adams (1744-1818)

These unhappy times call for the building of plans...that build from the bottom up and not from the top down, that put their faith once more in the forgotten man at the bottom of the economic pyramid.
- Franklin D. Roosevelt (1882-1945)

I must create a system, or be enslaved by another man's. I will not reason and compare: my business is to create.
- William Blake (1757-1827)

We prove what we want to prove, and the real difficulty is to know what we want to prove.
- Emile Auguste Chartier (1868-1951)

Money alone sets all the world in motion.
- Publilius Syrus (First century B.C.)

Ho, every one who thirsts, come to the waters; and he who has no money, come, buy and eat! Come, buy wine and milk without money and without price. Why do you spend your money for that which is not bread, and your labor for that which does not satisfy?
- Isaiah 55:1

If the doors of perception were cleansed everything would appear to man as it is, infinite.
- William Blake (1757-1827)

Democratic nations care little for what has been, but they are haunted by visions of what will be; in this direction their unbounded imagination grows and dilates beyond all measure.... Democracy, which shuts the past against the poet, opens the future before him.
- de Tocqueville (1805-1859)

Lend me the stone strength of the past, and I will lend you
The wings of the future, for I have them.
- Robinson Jeffers (1887-1962)

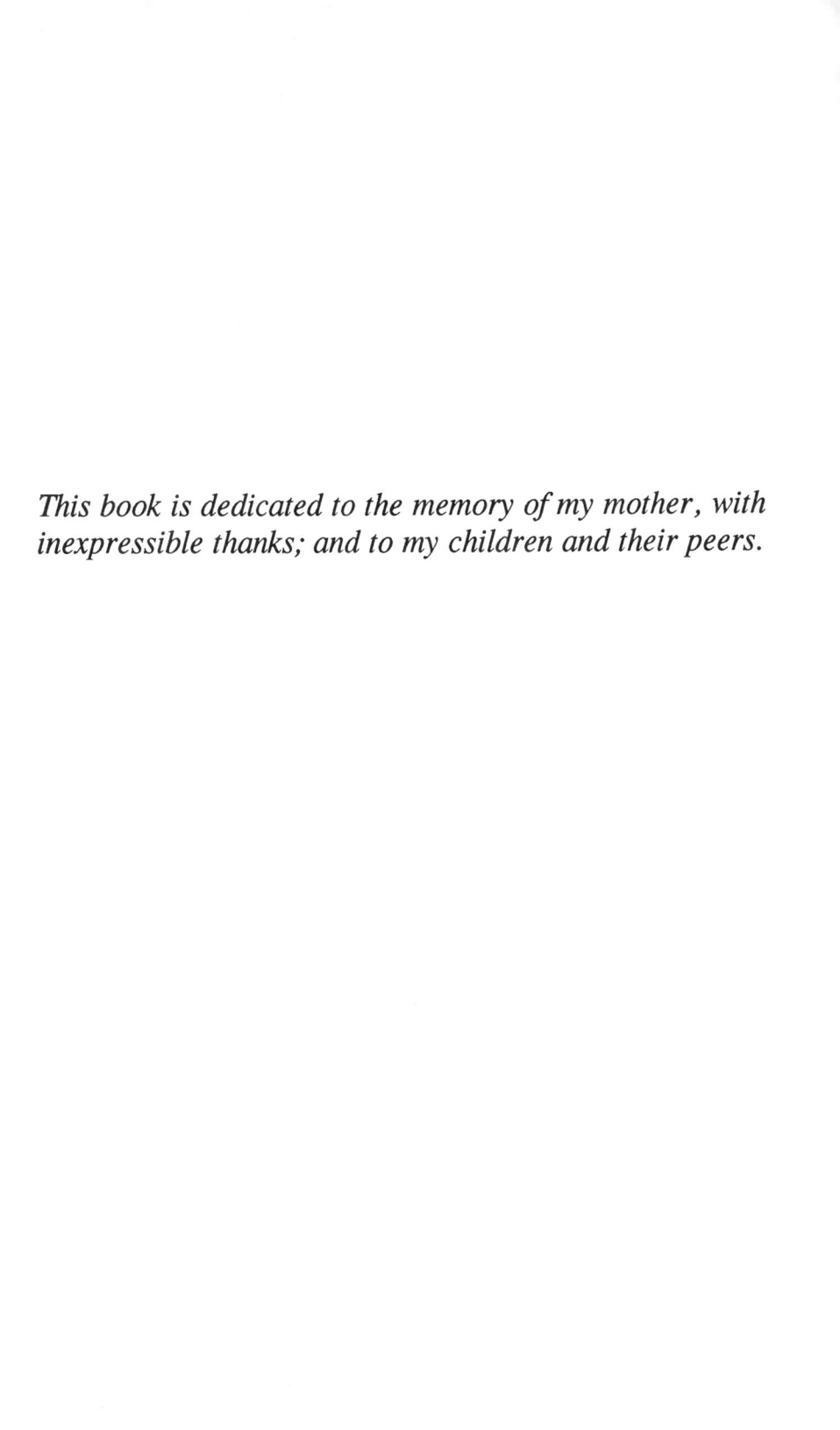

This book is dedicated to the memory of my mother, with inexpressible thanks; and to my children and their peers.

Copyright © 1993 by Vivian Arthur
All Rights Reserved

Library of Congress Catalog Card Number 93-071768

ISBN 0-9630804-1-5

Printed in the U.S.A.

Cover by Eric Velhagen/Reece Graphics Ltd.

The Apollo Press
P.O. Box 53207
Albuquerque, NM 87153

"Bringing You Quality Thought Since 1991"

THE INFINITE ECONOMY: HOW WE CAN ALL BE RICH

TABLE OF CONTENTS

INTRODUCTION..1
OUR ECONOMY..1
WHAT IS THE INFINITE ECONOMY?......................2
HOW WE CAN IMPLEMENT AN INFINITE
    ECONOMY...3
HERE'S THE CATCH: LIVELIHOODS.....................5
SKEPTIC'S CORNER: WHAT COULD STOP US, AND
    WHY IT SHOULDN'T..6

    1.   World Leaders Will Never Agree To It..............6
    2.   Rich People Won't Like It............................7
    3.   It's Inconsistent With Religion.....................8
    4.   Society Will Completely Fall Apart.................9
    5.   If We're All Rich We Would Have No
          Motivation to Do Anything..................11
    6.   Being Rich Will Make Us Disgustingly
          Gluttonous......................................12
    7.   Status Quo Inertia....................................13
    8.   It's Already Too Late................................14

WHY WE'RE READY TO BE RICH..........................15
WHAT COMMUNISM HAS TO DO WITH
    THIS..18
WHAT FREE MARKET CAPITALISM HAS TO
    DO WITH THIS..22
THE IMPLICATIONS OF AN INFINITE
    ECONOMY...25

    Livelihoods..25
    Caregiving...29
    Career Choice and Sincerity.............................31

Extinct Occupations..33
Health Care..35
Education...36
Working Conditions..38
Business Failure..39
Unemployment..41
Volunteerism..42
Generosity and Pity...43
Neuroses...45
Excuses...46
Criminality...47
Corporate Greed...52
Law..54
Governments..56
The Military...57
Immigration...59
Real Estate...59
Primitive Societies..61
Spiritual Search..62
Genius..65

TRANSACTIONS..66
DOES THE WHOLE WORLD HAVE TO AGREE TO AN INFINITE ECONOMY FOR IT TO WORK?..................67
WHAT AN INFINITE ECONOMY WON'T DO..68

INTRODUCTION

This book is about how we can efficiently eliminate the following problems from our reality: unemployment, the health care crisis, homelessness, the plight of Third World nations, poverty of all kinds, the welfare crisis, most crime, corporate greed, exploitation, unparented children, gender-based economic inequality, and a lot of bureaucracy. We have plenty of other problems that this solution will not address, but this solution will take away a big chunk of the ones we've got right now.
The solution is to make everybody rich.
This book explains how we can do it.

"Wine maketh merry: but money answereth all things."
- Ecclesiastes 10:19

OUR ECONOMY

Right now human beings operate an economy based on the premise that everything that has value fits within a finite pie. We have tried to remedy our social problems by dividing the pie into more equitable slices. At different periods of history in different locales the pie has grown and shrunk, but regardless of the size of the value pie, we have always regarded it as limited. It can run out. If you get a bigger slice of it, it appears that you are depriving someone else of their dinner, which is essentially true. Everyone, whether in possession of a generous or a skimpy slice, agrees with this conception of the world's wealth. Those individuals engaged in "creating wealth," even for a large group of people, still view a finite economy as self evident.

An economy, however, is not a material object with finite dimensions. It is instead a psychological event. The ring of limitations that we place around what we value is a mental one. It does not exist outside of our conception of it. Therefore we have it in our capacity to take the finite ring away, altering our way of viewing our economy, and thereby changing the way we live. We can all be rich. There is absolutely no law in the universe to stop us.

"The earth does not argue,
Is not pathetic, has no arrangements,
Does not scream, haste, persuade, threaten, promise,
Makes no discriminations, has no conceivable failures,
Closes nothing, refuses nothing, shuts none out."
- Walt Whitman (1819-1892)

WHAT IS THE INFINITE ECONOMY?

There is nothing particularly "real" about the way we run our economy right now; it is merely what has evolved from our premises about value and its limitations. If we change our premises about value, we set in motion new ways of exchanging value. It has become clear that our present system of economics serves very little of humanity - if indeed it serves anyone at all. If our axioms give us poor results, we shouldn't hesitate to change them to something that gives us positive and satisfying results.

The premise of an infinite economy is this: everybody is entitled to all the wealth they need. If we run out of money we just make more of it. Every adult citizen in our realm of existence can take as much as they want.

It sounds "too easy." It is. It can also work, and be as real as the economy we live with right now.

"Money is coined liberty, and so it is ten times dearer to a man who is deprived of freedom."
- Dostoevski (1821-1881)

THE INFINITE ECONOMY 3

"Give to every human being every right that you claim for yourself."
- Robert Ingersoll (1833-1899)

"The world is his, who has money to go over it."
- Ralph Waldo Emerson (1803-1882)

HOW WE CAN IMPLEMENT AN INFINITE ECONOMY

It has often been observed that if we could manage to get all the people in the world to agree to <u>anything</u>, most of our problems as a species would be over. To date, nobody has thought of anything we can all agree with about how people ought to live. We have drastically different opinions about how to relate to the divine mind (or if one exists at all), how to have a successful marriage, how to lead a moral life, how to raise kids, and so forth. We may be very far from agreement on those kinds of issues.

If there is one thing that we can come together and agree about, it is this: "It wouldn't bother me in the least to be a millionaire in a world of millionaires."

Under our present system it is naturally difficult for anyone with a conscience to enjoy the fruits of abundance while the inescapable evidence of human suffering is so unavoidable. In order for someone to be comfortable living in abundance, they must either live with a vague feeling of guilt or rationalize it away with such sentiments as "They could improve their lives if they wanted to," or "I am more deserving," or "My being poor wouldn't help them anyway," or "That's the way it is and there's really nothing I can do about it." The entire experience of abundance is psychologically tainted by our current system. This is the result of trying to divide up a finite pie.

THE INFINITE ECONOMY

We have already attempted to eradicate starvation and deprivations of all kinds by reapportioning shares of the pie, and this has never proved even remotely successful. If we instead make everybody rich, we not only eliminate the deprivations, we create an environment where abundance is free of its psychological drain and can therefore be enjoyed. By everyone.

This is how an infinite economy can be implemented:

The first step is making a common global currency. We can call it "The Coin of the Realm." Since it is a manufactured symbol of value, we can create as much of it as we want. This is no different in essence from what we are doing right now, in that when we are able to convince ourselves that something new is of sufficient worth we endow it with exchangeable value, and new wealth is created. In an infinite economy, we merely acknowledge that all value is nothing more than a psychological endowment and that any limits to it are our own. If instead of "gold" as our primary unit of value we decide that "citizenship in the known world" will do just as well, we have created an entirely new source of wealth. Every adult citizen of the planet in such an economy can go to the bank and get as much currency as they want.

Ideally, our world leaders would recognize the infinite economy as in the best interests of their respective constituencies and agree to the new, unlimited global currency. A date would be named, say January 1 of whatever year, for the institution of the new economy. We would be given sufficient time - a year or whatever - to consider the implications for ourselves and our businesses and to mentally prepare for the change.

Then, one New Year's Day we'll all wake up to find ourselves newly endowed with unlimited value within our sphere.

"There are no intrinsic reasons for the scarcity of capital."
- John Maynard Keynes (1883-1946)

THE INFINITE ECONOMY

"Money speaks sense in a language all nations understand."
- Aphra Behn (1640-1689)

"Not even the gods fight against necessity."
- The Seven Sages (c.650 - c. 550 B.C.)

HERE'S THE CATCH: LIVELIHOODS

There is one catch to creating a viable infinite economy, and it is this: everyone must have a livelihood. Every citizen in our newly abundant reality must contribute something to it, or the system will obviously fall apart. "Being rich" will be meaningless if it causes our global society to come to a standstill. In order to begin, we must all agree to set the system in motion while continuing to do what we're doing right now. That shouldn't be a burden to anyone, since every individual will suddenly be compensated for their efforts with unlimited funds. As we adjust to the new economy, we can gradually make changes through the channels that currently exist: want ads, networking, employment agencies, going into business for oneself, and so on. There will no doubt be businesses that can't handle more employees than they currently employ, but there will just as certainly be fields hungry for more contributors who haven't been able to afford them under the current system. We can start from where we are and gradually match talent and desire with needs, until we discover an equilibrium that both meets society's true needs and provides outlets for the actual talents of human beings.

The implementation of an infinite economy is based on the premise that it is possible to make a graceful and satisfying society out of things that human beings love to do, or at the very least don't mind a bit. If this should prove untenable, we're wasting our time being human.

SKEPTIC'S CORNER: WHAT COULD STOP US, AND WHY IT SHOULDN'T

As already mentioned, there exists no law in reality that would prevent us from changing our system of economics. There is nothing inevitable about the system we are using; it has merely evolved from our old premises. If we find ourselves unable to make change, then, it will be for human reasons, not divine ones. There exist possible objections to embracing an infinite economy, but none actually hold water. Here are some of them:

#1. WORLD LEADERS WILL NEVER AGREE TO IT

The purpose of having leaders at all is to galvanize the general population and unite its intents for the benefit of all. Our world leaders exist, then, to see to our needs and act in accordance with our desires. Most of the international problems we experience can be traced directly to attempts by our leaders to negotiate for our good - even if that negotiation is violent and based on nothing more than killing capacity. The leaders of every country are representatives put in place to perform the will of their specific groups. That being the case, there is no denying that an infinite economy is in the best interests of every population, with complete equitability, straight across the board. Once it is realized that an infinite economy is possible, and its extremely positive implications are known, its implementation becomes inevitable. Any leader unwilling to act in the interests of his or her group will be replaced by someone who will. In the case of the most corrupt officials - those who have no sincere interest in the aspirations of their populations and who exist in their capacities only to plunder from their charges - an infinite economy remains a logical choice. Even the most corrupt official is merely an individual "on the take" in a have-not world, and these individuals are generally frustrated by how much they lack. Shifting from a finite economy to an infinite one will satisfy their personal self-interest. Coincidentally, it will satisfy everyone else's, too.

#2. RICH PEOPLE WON'T LIKE IT

The infinite economy benefits everybody, regardless of current financial status, by providing every member of society with something absolutely unattainable under our present system: infinite wealth. Nobody has to give anything up, turn anything in, or surrender present wealth in any way. The infinite economy is a system whereby struggle and deprivation are eliminated where they exist, and everybody - rich or poor - ends up with more than they have now.

Imagine, however, that we do discover that there are people who are wealthy under the current system who believe that their worthiness is predicated on the suffering and poverty of others, people who balk at the idea of global abundance as a threat to their self image. Are we really intended to base our global financial premises on the fears of the spiritually immature? We should no more accept limiting, punishing, poisoning rules for our economic system than a group of ten year olds playing a game in the backyard should accept bizarre or patently unfair rules proposed by a four year old who wants to join their game. Mature and compassionate people of any economic strata abhor poverty and seek to remedy it. People who require the sight of the sufferings of others in order to attain some semblance of self esteem are merely little brothers and sisters who will grow and learn in their own season. They needn't be hated, insulted, or feared. But they certainly shouldn't be the people laying down the social rules of play.

#3. IT'S INCONSISTENT WITH RELIGION

In some religious traditions, earthly live is <u>supposed</u> to be arduous and unpleasant and filled with suffering: this is where we are meant to "prove our mettle" and our fitness for the afterlife. At first glance, then, an infinite economy may appear inconsistent with what some of us consider our spiritual purpose, particularly since many religious traditions regard money as debased or evil. These beliefs, however, arose because it appeared obvious that enjoying wealth <u>within a deprived system</u> was inconsistent with a developed, sympathetic conscience. Bringing an <u>unlimited</u> supply of money into the system changes that picture drastically.

One of the precepts of any system of religion is concern for the suffering of our fellows. To date this has taken the form of piecemeal assistance to the most obviously needy - indeed, there has thus far been no other way to go about the business of relieving suffering. If it is spiritually acceptable - even highly desirable - for human beings to assist the needy, then certainly eliminating that suffering entirely must be compatible with a spiritual life. In fact, dispensing with the need to focus on lack of money may well clear the way for a more profound spiritual life in a substantial portion of the population.

There are cultures that shun materialism, and there is absolutely no reason why access to money should mean a turn to flagrant acquisitiveness. Communities are free to live in accordance with their spiritual beliefs; there will be no one standing by to insist that the money be spent. The existence of free-flowing and endless money will only ensure that every option is available to all members of society. Its use is at each individual's personal discretion.

An infinite economy will actually force religious organizations to demonstrate what they are truly made of. They won't plead for your money, because they can have as much as they want. An infinite economy will make the business of our spiritual institutions spirituality. They will be newly free to fulfill their stated purpose and hopefully enrich our lives to far greater degrees. Lastly, in response to the idea that the purpose of human life is suffering and nothing else, a steady and equitable flow of money to everyone won't prevent humanity from bearing the weight of its many other problems, or even creating new ones, if that's what we want to do. Suffering will remain an option, if it really seems worthwhile to anyone.

"I want nothing to do with any religion concerned with keeping the masses satisfied to live in hunger, filth, and ignorance. I want nothing to do with any order, religious or otherwise, which does not teach people that they are capable of becoming happier and more civilized, on this earth, capable of becoming true man, master of his fate and captain of his soul."
- Jawaharlal Nehru (1889-1964)

#4.   SOCIETY WILL COMPLETELY FALL APART

In a free market society a certain balance is achieved between supply and demand; that is, in fact, the stated goal of a free market system. We use money as feedback that tells us whether or not we're on the right track and serving our society appropriately. It's true that huge numbers of people do work they dislike and contribute nothing of enduring value to society, but the free market system works for the most part and we may fear to monkey with it in any kind of substantial way. We're afraid that a new system won't equilibrate and everything we may have gained through progress will completely fall apart. Because our present system serves us, we're afraid that it's the only possible system able to do so. This is not true. There are probably an infinite number of potential systems that would reach a satisfying equilibrium in just the way our present one does, if not more so. The infinite economy is one of these. It absorbs free market principles, in that our endeavors will continue to be based upon supply and demand. What is different is the subjective agreement we'll be using to generate our seemingly objective reality.

All socio-economic systems have a subjective basis. They are group decisions about what has value and what doesn't. These decisions are constantly changing and evolving through time as our ideas about value change. For example, a torturer working for Torquemada was valued, while a torturer in present day America goes to jail. We're always revising our opinions about value, in ways both big and small. It is those sort of opinions - always subjective and mutable - that result in a social system that appears iron-clad and objective to the individual. When we change our ideas about value, society changes. This is what we're doing right now. It is what we have always done. And it is all we have to do to generate a new system that will be as balanced and as objectively real-seeming as the one we use now or any other in the entire course of history. All we have to do is change our minds.

"I know no safe depository of the ultimate powers of the society but the people themselves; and if we think them not enlightened enough to exercise their control with a wholesome discretion, the remedy is not to take it from them, but to inform their discretion by education."
- Thomas Jefferson (1743-1826)

#5. IF WE'RE ALL RICH WE WOULD HAVE NO MOTIVATION TO DO ANYTHING

In America today people are motivated by a promised compensation of $4.25 an hour to do meaningless work that they hate and to perform the will of superiors, however distasteful. The reason that they are willing to do this is the fear of losing the $4.25. With such conditions already part of our reality, how can we imagine that compensation of unlimited funds combined with a fear of having to abandon the system that produces those funds will fail to motivate people? We will find ourselves willing - even joyously eager - to contribute to a system that provides for us on such an abundant scale. Tasks that may presently seem unpleasant or lowly will look very different when they are highly valued. The only tasks that will be unbearable will be truly meaningless ones, in that they make no real contribution to our society and no one wants to do them. Those sort of tasks will vanish from our work environments, leaving us only with those jobs that are necessary and those that people love to do. Working won't be a humiliating occasion to grit one's teeth and bear it; we will instead have the satisfaction of knowing that our contributions have meaning either in terms of satisfying true and basic needs of society or in terms of enhancing it with brilliance, beauty, and human genius.

An infinite economy will create a society worth our cooperation and contribution. Our current society keeps most of our citizens on an exhausting treadmill for the privilege of eating and living in a house. If people are willing to spend their lives struggling for food and shelter, there is no doubt that people will be willing to address their abilities to the needs of society in return for complete freedom from economic worries of any kind.

"Follow your desire as long as you live and do not perform more than is ordered; do not lessen the time of following desire, for the wasting of time is an abomination to the spirit.... When riches are gained, follow desire, for riches will not profit if one is sluggish."
- Ptahhotpe (Twenty-fourth century B.C.)

"Follow your bliss."
- Joseph Campbell (1904-1987)

#6. BEING RICH WILL MAKE US DISGUSTINGLY GLUTTONOUS

Insecurity is the root of greed. If a person is offered a nice breakfast and is completely certain that lunch and dinner will be coming later in the day, there is no need for gorging. Our current system leaves the vast majority of people so uncertain of their future that it seems logical and prudent to take everything offered, even to extreme and gluttonous degrees.

When lack of money is no longer a threat or even a possibility, people will be able to relax and focus upon other aspects of their lives. Our psychological neediness will be removed and we won't feel pathologically compelled to acquire. We will instead begin to consider what we are, what we like to do, what type of talents and abilities we have to be developed. Rabid acquisitiveness will no longer have meaning in a world where absolutely everyone could acquire endlessly if they wanted to. What will begin to matter is not what you own - everybody can own - but what you can think and do and contribute. An infinite economy will free us from the frantic gathering of objects and allow us to discover what we really are.

THE INFINITE ECONOMY

If it should actually happen that we grant humanity unlimited means and the result is that everyone is interested only in acquiring objects to grotesque proportions, then we will have to face the fact that this is what a freed humanity is and this is how humanity expresses itself in its emancipation. It would hardly be something to be proud of, but finding out what we truly are is still worthwhile, and we should give ourselves freedom to know it. The chances remain great that we would discover that we are something much more interesting than gluttons.

> "Industrialized communities neglect the very objects for which it is worth while to acquire riches in their feverish preoccupation with the means by which riches can be acquired."
> - Richard Henry Tawney (1880-1962)

#7. STATUS QUO INERTIA

There is comfort in the familiar. It is often easier to do nothing than to find purpose and make changes in our reality, however beneficial those changes might appear. There are certainly people who are plenty comfortable with things just as they are, people who may well see no reason for changing anything, and those people tend to be the ones who currently have the power to make or to withhold the change.

It's true that we don't have to change anything. We can continue to slap band-aids on our problems as they arise and to try to solve them from within the very system that caused them in the first place. We can perceive a painless solution for them, nod to the solution, ignore it, and keep doing exactly what we're doing right now.

But if we're offered a solution so simple and so sweeping, and we choose not to insist on its implementation, there can be only one conclusion to draw: we actually like it just how it is. The way we do things is how human beings choose to live. But we must then acknowledge that voting to continue on our present course is humanity's choice. We are responsible for it.

Reality reflects the desires of its participants. If we like things how they are, we can certainly keep at it. Starvation, deprivation, suffering, and struggle can just be part of "being human." Or we can choose a course that allows us to be human in a whole new way. Once we know that reality can be handled differently, the responsibility for our living conditions is our own.

#8. IT'S ALREADY TOO LATE

The history of the human race is so rife with violence, starvation, atrocity, frustration, exploitation, and injustice that it may appear that there's no way to save or even improve ourselves. The people alive now are so enured to the hardships of the finite system of economics that it may be difficult, if not impossible, to imagine that we possess the goodness of heart, sympathy, compassion, and equanimity that it would take to free ourselves from deprivation and make the new system float. We've become cold-hearted, sick of the pleas from the homeless and disadvantaged, cynical about our institutions and each other, bored by the prisoners we stuff into our jails, and generally unable to cope with the release that abundance would bring.

Maybe so. We have no way of knowing what we're made of because so far we haven't been free to be it. Perhaps the system we've created has so brow-beaten us that we've been rendered feelingless and essentially worthless.

But let's find that out for ourselves. Let's see if that's true. If it is, and we discover that we truly are unable to cope with an infinite economy, then we will have discovered where our limits lie. We will know that we drove ourselves straight to a dead end, and we can decide what to do about it then. We may, of course, discover instead that we're just heartbroken from living under a trying system, and that we're actually in fine shape and completely capable of dreaming up and executing a graceful and worthwhile society.

WHY WE'RE READY TO BE RICH

"When I was a child we didn't have VCR's, microwaves, camcorders, CD players, video games, automated teller machines, computers, calculators...." Any living adult can make this sort of statement. People alive today had a massive amount of technology dumped into their laps, and suddenly things unimaginable only ten years earlier were simply an unremarkable part of our lives. As these innovations were introduced to us, we welcomed them and adjusted to them with ease. We have therefore demonstrated our ability and willingness to assimilate even the most dramatic changes in a very short time, provided that those changes improve or enrich our lives with little or no down-side.

Since instituting an infinite economy certainly meets the criteria of improving and enriching our lives without asking us to surrender anything significant that we love, we are fortunate to already have a model for its assimilation - a model of easy welcome that many of us have already experienced through the advent of the new technologies. We know how to cope with change, even drastic change. We've had a practice run, so to speak, and discovered that handling new ways of doing things is something that we can accomplish gracefully. We can view the coming of an infinite economy with the same sense of wonder and excitement that we experienced as our technologies were ushered into our lives. The technology model is extremely reassuring and useful, but our readiness for a new system of economics extends into even more profound realms of human evolution, and technology plays a role here too: The much-heralded global village is actually upon us. Since The Beatles serenaded us worldwide with "All You Need Is Love" via satellite, we've come to take global broadcasts for granted. As our technology has improved, our interest in and knowledge of each other has blossomed. We "know what's out there" in a way our ancestors - even our own parents - never could. We have been confronted with our human similarities and the knowledge of our relatedness again and again, thanks to our technologies.

The Founding Fathers of America had what they perceived as a new chunk of land on which to try their political experiment, where they could proceed freshly and with no taint of the old monarchical ways. Today the world is explored, mapped, settled, and known. There is no mysterious new real estate on the other side of any ocean; we already know what we'll find when we get there. We are therefore unable to stake out new territory for the purposes of attempting to improve our living conditions with new social systems. Any journeys we make with an idea of improving our lives must now be inward ones. We're familiar with the contours of the plant; it's time to acquaint ourselves with the contours of ourselves and seek to develop and improve our lives using the riches that lay buried in that infinite territory.

There is one other aspect of our lives that demonstrates our state of preparation for a new economic system: debt. We're all familiar with the concept of national debt, and most of us are familiar with personal debt as well. Debt is obviously a feature of a finite economy, in that it presumes a limited amount of means. Loans were never treated as surplus money that could be handed about freely. Our systems of generating and handling debt have seemed as self-evident as the finite economy that spawned them. This all worked just fine when debt existed at relatively manageable levels; no seams showed that would indicate that our financial presumptions were psychological and therefore nebulous. This was true even a decade or two ago. We believed in debt. Since that time, however, our debt pictures on both personal and national levels have become absolutely ludicrous. Now that we have vaulted beyond smallish, manageable debt levels it becomes evident that the concept of debt makes no sense. We've invented tools such as bankruptcy laws to cope with the reality that we can't get blood from a stone, a reaction to the sure knowledge that no creditor ever got his money back from a guy sitting in debtor's prison. Once money is given, spent, and gone, there exists no power in the universe to force it to come back.

When we consider things like "your share of the national debt," that debt becomes unreal and even laughable. Will any of us, most of whom are living hand-to-mouth, _ever_ be able to ante up our "share"? Absolutely not. Debt has caused the finite economy to fall apart. We can either continue to believe in that economic system and scrape along and struggle accordingly, or we can call an end to that particular (and clearly flawed) way of doing things, and institute a system that provides us with the possibility of quality lives.

With every year our fates as individuals become more and more tied to our inter-relatedness as nations. We can sit and watch while the world economy as currently created sputters and dies, or we can step in now and change the game.

"I have been poor and I have been rich. Rich is better."
- Sophie Tucker (1884-1966)

WHAT COMMUNISM HAS TO DO WITH THIS

We've spent the better part of a century struggling to determine whether a communistic or a capitalistic system of economics is "better." We spent a lot of time glaring at each other and waving weapons of destruction in each other's faces. Each side, instead of just leaving the other alone to find out if the system was decent, basically agreed that the "better" system would be the system that could generate the most weaponry within it. Those were the agreed terms of the game: More killing power equals better system of economics. Aside from the underlying absurdity of the terms (killing power in reality says nothing about the quality of an economic system), this contest also had the additional drawback of siphoning large shares of finite means into devices that, if ever actually used, would in all likelihood extinct all of us. The arms race was basically a nonsense game, the result of which told us very little about the economic questions it purported to answer. However, once the terms were agreed upon, neither side was willing to forfeit, and we diligently continued the game in a "winner-take-all" fashion.

The free market capitalistic system won this game. It is now regarded as the "better" system, and communism to a large degree lies in rubble. Many see this as a victory of good over evil. Communism is viewed as vanquished worthlessness. Since we set it up as a battle between the forces of good and evil, it may even appear that the intense bruising we gave our own economy in the name of the contest, and the suffering we generated from it, are well worth it, given the stakes. Communism lost. It is now history. There is nothing to salvage from the wreckage.

THE INFINITE ECONOMY

What was worthwhile about the idea of communism is its resonance with our sympathies for the victims of our unjust system. Drastic inequalities among the citizens of the world were - and are - quite plain. Communism, far from being deliberately evil, is based on a big-hearted impulse: the eradication of the obvious social inequalities. The way communism has been put into practice is seriously flawed - so much so that it unraveled. That doesn't mean that the impulse that generated it should be discarded, or that we should all feel free to just shrug and deal with the suffering of capitalism's "victims" as necessary to the greater good. An infinite economy can take what was brilliant about communism - its impulse toward equality, sharing, and social justice - and discard its flaws. The great experiment of communism on our planet need not have been in vain and its sufferings meaningless. Any new solution should always synthesize two factions that had previously appeared incompatible or even at war with one another; this is what the infinite economy can do. It can satisfy the most liberal and the most conservative ends of the spectrum.

Communism's chief flaw was the agreement to all be poor together. It didn't seem right for anyone to have a bigger slice of a finite pie - it still doesn't to many - and within a communistic system this was dealt with by handing out puny slices to all, satisfying no one. What's more, exact equality is utterly impractical, and it inevitably became clear that some within the system had more than others anyhow - not something likely to please a population trying to eke out a meal from a puny slice. The infinite economy recognizes that inequality will exist, that slices of the pie come in all sizes - but when you're working from an infinite pie, every slice is a smaller or larger infinity. That turns inequality into a hearty and welcome diversity.

It's interesting to contemplate what the outcome of the capitalist/communist battle would have been if the communists had chosen to all be rich together instead, working with infinity. The Soviet Union was large and diverse enough to have designed an infinite system, and it may well have found other impoverished nations anxious to join their society of millionaires, thus enriching their access to talent and resources. People from systems unwilling to switch to infinity might have been anxious to emigrate, enriching them again. They could have rolled their eyes at the weapons that capitalists waved at them and refused to involve themselves in military initiatives. History might have been very different if communism had taken abundance as its premise rather than want. Today we might have had victorious communists scoffing at the greedy economic contests that finally felled capitalism.

That obviously didn't happen, and one of the reasons that it didn't was communism's glorification of the <u>worker</u>. This was inconsistent with our aspirations as humans; we don't want to just be "workers" and pat ourselves on the back about it. There are a lot more aces in the hand that humans have been dealt as a species, and these are the sources of our genuine pride. In comparison with our humanly geniuses, our ability to work hardly seems like something to crow about.

It's true that having workers is substantially superior to having slaves. Having workers must have appeared sufficiently superior to a system based on enslavement that communists were moved to applaud it. Having workers, however, isn't enough. Communism stopped to shout "hooray" too soon. An infinite economy can make us something even better than workers: we can be contributors, and our contribution can be our individual genius.

Another flaw of communism as practiced was the attempt to legislate livelihoods. This presumes that every human would hate to do the things that most needed to be done, and that the society itself was so unappealing that willing contributors to it would not rise up and volunteer their services. The result was a complete crushing of the human desire for self-knowledge and expression in accordance with that knowledge. Few people could be what they suspected they'd be good at. An infinite economy encourages individual genius and contribution; we need it all. It is premised on faith in humanity's ability to fill its own needs, humanity's capacity to flower out of what we are.

A third flaw of communism was its rejection of a spiritual aspect to life. Human beings are multidimensional, and our spiritual institutions seek to articulate dimensions that lie beneath the most surface and obvious ones. Again, "work," being a surface endowment, doesn't begin to reflect our actual dimensionality, and its worship leaves a population spiritually impoverished. A positive feature of the infinite economy, while itself utterly secular, is the freeing up of our spiritual institutions from their roles as beggars. Our spiritual institutions can experience a renaissance of exploration into human dimensionality and let us know their findings.

Free market capitalism won its battle with communism. That doesn't necessarily mean that the system as it is currently practiced is the final answer to our human desires. It just means that the battle itself is ended, and we can get on with the business of improving our world using the best of everything that humans have so far expressed, and coming up with much, much more.

"Communism is a judgment on our failure to make democracy real and to follow through on the revolutions that we initiated."
- Martin Luther King, Jr. (1929-1968)

"Capitalism, it is said, is a system wherein man exploits man. And communism - it is vice versa."
- Daniel Bell

"Man alone can enslave man."
- Simone Weil (1909-1943)

WHAT FREE MARKET CAPITALISM HAS TO DO WITH THIS

A free market economy is based on competition, on "making the grade." The game goes like this: You see if you can get people to value what you have to offer. If they value your offering, they surrender some of their money to you. You collect the money from your valuers and use it to create a lifestyle that reflects your degree of societal valuation. Some people - not necessarily those most successful at it - love this game. Others aren't interested in it in the least. Some arrive here, for any number of reasons, with an inability to play it at all, or with a starting hand so paltry that their chances of succeeding in the game are almost nil. As practiced, a free market economy responds to this by saying "tough luck - this is the only game in town." This attitude fills our streets with the homeless and the needy, and we regard this condition as an unfortunate but necessary element of the system. You can't run a competition if you don't end up with losers.

An infinite economy allows an unlimited number of games and contests for the competitors among us: we can find out who can write great books, invent innovative products, run the fastest, devise exciting educational institutions, make stunning movies, solve our ecological problems, build the most gorgeous homes, and so on. The winners of these contests can even say "Ha ha - I did it - I'm the best" if they want to. But the price of losing will no longer be starvation. Human beings like to excel. One of the ways we push ourselves to our limits is the use of competition. There is nothing inherently wrong with it, as it often takes us to new levels we didn't know we could reach. What *is* wrong is our manner of rewarding our deserving victors and casting off their honorable competitors. An infinite economy leaves everybody secure about their honor and their value, thereby encouraging everyone who wants to to play their hardest and to take the kind of risks that open whole new fields of endeavor and bring new pockets of knowledge to people. For our citizens who may have other priorities than contests, people more interested in raising a family and making meaningful and necessary contributions to their communities, for example, we can reassure them of our respect for their worth. Because we need them, too.

The materialistic society that free market capitalism generates is often spoken of in very derogatory terms with words like "shallow" or "empty." It is no doubt true that many free market citizens become so involved in keeping pace with the game and its material prizes that many other brilliant aspects of their own natures are left to stagnate. But there is a positive aspect to the sort of material focus a free market economy generates, an aspect that will serve us well in an infinite economy.

The proliferation of consumer choice has had the effect of forcing the citizens of consumerist societies to constantly ask: what do I prefer? What kind of person am I? Do I like Colgate or Crest, Coke or Pepsi, Levis or Wranglers? Do I shop at boutiques or department stores? What furniture do I think is the most attractive? What color would I like my house to be? How do I like to wear my hair? What books and magazines do I like to read? What music moves me? And on and on and on. From the biggest to the tiniest detail of our lives, we are offered a choice, again and again and again. We are asked to define ourselves, to think about what appeals to us, and to come to know ourselves and our preferences in a detail that is sumptuous and exquisite. A consumerist society doesn't let you "just pick something"; you always have to decide. Even our poorest citizens participate in this on a daily basis, as they go about fulfilling the needs and wants that they are able to answer. Choice is everywhere.

And what this has done is given us tremendous skill at creating ourselves. We've learned to ask ourselves an unending series of questions about what is "better" from our individual perspective, and to synthesize ourselves from those decisions. We're constantly creating and re-creating ourselves out of what we're offered.

Self-knowledge and self-creation are indispensable to an infinite economy. These skills are what will make a society based on such an economy colorful, expressive, and satisfying. We may not want to continue to focus on our self expressions through such blatantly material channels. But materialism is what taught us to do it at all.

> "My reading of Marx also convinced me that truth is found neither in Marxism nor in the traditional capitalism. Each represents a partial truth. Historically, capitalism failed to see the truth in collective enterprise, and Marxism failed to see the truth in individual enterprise."
> - Martin Luther King, Jr. (1929-1968)

THE IMPLICATIONS OF AN INFINITE ECONOMY

"But it is pretty to see what money will do."
- Samuel Pepys (1633-1703)

LIVELIHOODS

Many people today hate their jobs. There are a number of reasons for this. First, many of the positions available to people are clearly meaningless, in that they enrich neither the person performing them nor the society at large. They exist for the sole purpose of money generation, for the worker and for the company, and add nothing whatever of substance or quality to anyone's life. People are willing to accept all manner of mindless tasks because the option is unbearable: the inability to eat, and homelessness. These conditions make the drudgery of meaningless work appear necessary.

Most people have some idea of what they would really enjoy doing; they have aspirations. Yet most remain locked into meaningless employment because of the risk involved in breaking out of it: the stakes are simply too high. It's not a case of laziness, since people trapped in these kinds of jobs work as hard or harder than the most successful among us. They do difficult things for long hours and receive little compensation for it. This can hardly be termed "lazy," especially when we consider how heartbreaking and painful meaningless work is to the people who perform it. The price we pay to avoid hunger is huge. And it doesn't have to be. In fact, it shouldn't be.

It's hard to look at the way we handle things today and not conclude that we hate ourselves. We make ourselves struggle to attain things that the earth itself provides for free. We have people who love to seed the earth and tend to its growth. We have people who love to prepare and serve food. We have people who love to design dwellings, and people who love to build them. For every actual human need, there are people who can take satisfaction in its answer. Instead of paying attention to our needs and their satisfactions, we screw around with constructing idiotic job roles <u>around</u> the needs so that they can be answered. There's a step in there that we not only don't require, we actually waste our lives dwelling on it.

In an infinite economy it will evolve that there are only two types of livelihoods: those absolutely necessary for human survival, and those that bring joy to people and enrich our communities. Any other type of work will gradually - if not immediately - go away. Everyone will be performing work that matters, and will be a millionaire for it.

Consider an example: the fast food industry. Right now the people participating in this type of employment are the low-paid people running the cash register and flipping the burgers, and the franchise holders who were attracted to the industry because it offered the possibility of a comfortable amount of money. The infinite economy gives this simple test to everyone involved: would you still do it if you were a millionaire? Would the franchise holders actually wish to run that particular type of establishment, would they rather start the restaurant of their dreams, or would they rather be in another line of work entirely? Would the cooks still want to prepare that type of food, would they prefer preparing a better quality meal, or is there something else that appeals to them more? If money were no object, would the patrons want to eat the fast food, or would they instead visit the new restaurant a former franchise holder started and eat food made by people who really enjoyed making it?

If millionaires want to run fast food restaurants and work in them and eat in them, then we'll have them. If millionaires have another idea for something they like better, fast food chains will disappear. In either case, whatever we end up having will reflect the way that people who are completely free like to do things. The effect of this will be job satisfaction, pride in our work, and quality everywhere we turn. If we do have fast food, it will be because we truly enjoy it. If we don't truly enjoy it, it will disappear. All industries will face this test. The ones that pass it will serve the population in a quality manner and be staffed by satisfied people who like what they do. Human beings are diverse enough that we can safely assume that every need has a talent that answers it and every talent has a need it can fill.

What about the type of positions that are now considered "lowly" and distasteful but are things that society actually needs? We can live happy lives without telemarketers, but not without trash collectors.

The answer to this lies with people who are motivated to answer a community's needs, who can find satisfaction in the knowledge that their work is crucial to society. So many of our present occupations seem drab and uninspiring because they contribute nothing of substance to anyone. Many people who are locked into work they find dull would be more than happy to: (1) Do work they know has meaning, and (2) Be a millionaire because of it. The knowledge that we're helping to create a society abundant to both ourselves and our fellows is no small satisfaction. Even people with the very highest aspirations may well desire to contribute necessary work to their community for the sake of keeping such a splendid system afloat.

A good way to handle this might be through an "S.O.S. Newsletter." When a community finds itself in need of someone to perform a job crucial to its citizens, it could advertise the need in the newsletter and attract candidates interested in responding to an S.O.S. An infinite economy asks us to respond to our generous impulses rather than our selfish ones. Since it allows every citizen to be secure in the knowledge that their basic needs will be met and scrambling to get life's necessities is no longer necessary, the desperation that motivates selfishness will atrophy and die. An infinite economy creates a society worth our contribution.

Human beings do and always will admire skill and genius. This means that an infinite economy will not be without elements of prestige. Anyone who does something novel or amazing will be admired and honored by their peers. There will be a lot of room for aspiration.

We will not, however, have people choosing their livelihoods merely for prestige the way we do now. Prestige is currently tied to earning power, and this will obviously no longer be the case. Today we have people who decide to be doctors because they feel it is the best way to reap the maximum amount of prestige and money from their intelligence. In an infinite economy the only people attracted to such a profession will be those who want to apply their intelligence to healing, and for no other reason. Prestige and money will no longer be motivators, replaced with talent, interest, and the needs of the community. We won't see qualified medical practitioners select plastic surgery as their field for the sake of money; if we have plastic surgeons it will be because we have people who really want to be plastic surgeons and people who really want their services.

In short, the infinite economy will demand that everyone live in accordance with their real desires and aspirations. It wouldn't be far from the truth, in fact, to say that the infinite economy will require us to live in accordance with our wildest dreams.

"If we are to achieve a richer culture, rich in contrasting values, we must recognize the whole gamut of human potentialities, and so weave a less arbitrary social fabric, one in which each diverse human gift will find a fitting place."
- Margaret Mead (1901-1978)

CAREGIVING

Caregiving, as a necessity for society, is obviously a livelihood. Meeting the needs of people unable to care for themselves is one of the basic imperatives of any functioning society. This would include raising children, caring for an elderly parent, tending to a sick family member, or seeing to the needs of citizens disabled in any way, whether members of our own family or someone else's. Caregiving need not be the only livelihood one chooses. But it can be. It's needed.

In this way an infinite economy recognizes female genius in a way a finite economy never could. To call caregiving a "female genius" is not to say that only females can do it, and it's not to say that every female must do it. Caregiving is a female genius because it is one of the arts developed by females and still practiced to a large degree by females.

The economic system in place now almost completely ignores caregiving as an occupation, in that it seldom involves money, and when it does that money is usually quite low. It's impossible to say whether or not this state of affairs was inevitable, but it is clearly the way that things have evolved. We honor soldiers who stand ready to kill our enemies, we support them with public funds, we throw them a parade, and if they stand ready to kill for 20 years we give them financial support for the rest of their lives and say that they have "served their country." Contrast this attitude with the one that we offer to economically disadvantaged mothers trying to raise their own children and in need of public funds to do it: we sneer at them, tell them to "get a job," and call them "Welfare Queens." There's no parade, no pension after 20, 30, or 40 years of service. Yet raising children is something necessary to society: if these women don't do it, someone else has to. This is not always the case with our armed forces.

This is in no way meant to disparage the role our military has played, and it is not to imply that soldiers do not serve their country. This is only to illustrate that women raising children do too, and are not valued in our society for doing so. The fact that people are still willing to forfeit economic freedom for the sake of raising their own children or caring for their parents is remarkable: how many other occupations would still have willing participants if they paid nothing at all? This speaks for the inherent value of caregiving that is known deep within the souls of those who choose it. Faced with an economic system that assigns no value at all to this art, people still opt for it.

In a finite economy, caregiving leaves one economically vulnerable. As this becomes more and more clear, and as more and more caregivers had this truth driven home to them personally, a solution to the obvious injustice was sought. Not surprisingly, looking for a solution within the system that caused the problem was all anyone thought to do. The result has been catastrophic for one of the most worthwhile experiences in human possibility: love.

Our attempt to eliminate this drastic economic inequality was to encourage women to go get their own money, for only armed with money could a woman be impervious to the vulnerabilities of caregiving. We came to the conclusion that women couldn't afford love, couldn't afford trust, couldn't afford the "luxury" of acting as guides to their own children, even if their hearts yearned for love, trust, and motherhood. Under our system of economics, this appeared quite true. But a society that just has to "do without" love, trust, and the nurturing of our little ones is a very sad and perverse one indeed. Certainly no one should have to function as a caregiver, but for those whose hearts incline in that direction, the risk of destitution should not be part of the equation. We presently have women who stay married to abusive men for the sake of feeding and clothing their children. It's a pathetic payback for an impulse so selfless and heroic. An infinite economy encourages noble choices by eliminating their price and replacing that price with the means to create quality environments from which quality people can bloom.

CAREER CHOICE AND SINCERITY

It is absolutely imperative that there be no bureaucratic dictation of livelihoods. We have to allow ourselves to design a society out of what we have to offer, combined with what we need, enjoy, and appreciate. This way we not only give ourselves the ability to discover what humanity is really like, we also arrange it so that everywhere we go we encounter sincere people. We won't have to fear that our doctor is referring us for tests just to line his own pockets or to help out a friend. We won't need to be on guard at the car dealership because we fear that the salesman has his own agenda due to pressure from higher-ups. The mechanic won't lie to us to get hold of a few extra bucks. Nobody will have any incentive to lay hands on your money; they won't need it. Everyone's function will be to honestly do the job they're there to do. We will encounter nothing but honest employees. We will actually have the opportunity to trust each other with no risk of getting "ripped off."
What's more, we'll no longer encounter surly and disgusted people who loathe their jobs. Even the waitress pouring your

coffee will be a millionaire, and if she hated her job she'd go do something else. If she ever starts hating it, she will.

Since the infinite economy encourages us to actualize our dreams, we will no doubt discover that it is a pleasure to participate in one another's best fantasies. Living on grudgingly bestowed tips in a seedy diner may be unpleasant, but being a millionaire for passing out desserts in a gorgeous restaurant won't. We'll be handsomely compensated for taking part in other people's idea of fun, or making up our own fun and getting other people in on it.

One of the most horrific aspects of our present economic system is the way it stratifies participants according to their salaries. Bosses and subordinates are essentially antagonists working for opposite interests: bosses want the most work for the least pay, and subordinates want the most pay for the least work. Such a dynamic makes no one happy and poisons the work environment, completely disrupting any possibility of graceful and efficient productivity, and making job satisfaction difficult for anyone to achieve. Resentment proliferates, and the work environment becomes something to dread.

In an infinite economy, everybody is paid the same (infinity), so that work environments are places where people with common goals come together to achieve them. The staff of any company will consist of people interested in realizing the same vision and willing to do their part to make it happen. Bosses won't have to deal with disgruntled employees, and employees won't have to take crap from their bosses. Any relationship that proves unsatisfactory can be terminated without devastating effects for either side. It'll just be "on to the next thing."

"My lack of faith in the majority is dictated by my faith in the potentialities of the individual. Only when the latter

becomes free to choose his associates for a common purpose, can we hope for order and harmony out of this world of chaos and inequality."
- Emma Goldman (1869-1940)

EXTINCT OCCUPATIONS

Some of our present industries will die out for lack of interest. These will tend to be the ones that offer junk product to people who can't afford quality and that employ people desperate for money. Since we will no longer have citizens who can't afford quality or who need the money, they will disappear. We will stop inventing bogus industries in order to create wealth, and we will use our abundant wealth and talent for things that matter and that we like.

Other industries will simply no longer be needed. The insurance industry springs immediately to mind, and its demise will not only represent the death of something nebulous, it will free us from the curse of fear-mongering for profit.

It's not pleasant to consider that we might get cancer, break our leg, crash our car, watch our house burn down, or lose a beloved spouse. These are all unpleasant possibilities that an infinite economy won't eliminate. They could happen, and it's bad enough to have to worry about this sort of misfortune. But our insurance industries don't ask us to think about all of the catastrophes that could befall us, they ask us to imagine the catastrophes <u>and</u> our financial ruin. We don't just cope with having cancer, we cope with having cancer that also ruins us financially. We don't just mourn our spouse, we mourn our spouse and are poor. The insurance industry plays on our fears of misfortune coupled with the prospect of poverty, and then asks us to bet against ourselves. The insurance industry says "Lots of people get cancer and can't afford the treatment. We bet it won't be you." We envision it in all its ghastly detail until it's really clear, and when we generate sufficient fear we say "I bet it will be me," and hand over our money. If we don't get cancer, we lose our bet and thus our money. If we do get cancer, we deal with an extremely trying life crisis. Either way, we lose.

The insurance industry offers this perverse lose-or-lose proposition and flourishes, but this isn't its only downside. There are indications that powerfully visualizing events may actually assist their materialization, and this particular industry provides us with an endless parade of catastrophes to imagine. If they never do happen, we have at the very least spent some chunk of a finite lifetime dwelling on the idea that they might. This is a completely unconstructive use of human creativity.

Does anyone really want to sell fear? Of course not. The entire industry exists as an attempt by its participants to feed their families or to "get ahead" in a world where money can be mighty hard to come by. Insurance never cured cancer, prevented your automobile accident, or brought your spouse back to life; it only protected you from the financial implications of those catastrophes. We will no longer require that kind of protection and will be free to pour our energies into the problems themselves. The talented people now involved in the insurance industry might instead work on cures for diseases, improve auto safety, rebuild houses that burn down, or offer counsel to the bereaved. In other words, we can rechannel our energies into developing real solutions for our problems instead of making bets about who is likely to experience them. We will also make it so that nobody has to wave ugly pictures of tragedies in our faces for their supper.

Other extinct occupations will involve the wealth creation industries, which include investment professionals, fund raisers, stockbrokers, and the like. These people are presently involved

THE INFINITE ECONOMY

with trying to expand the money available with the finite pie, and there will no longer be a need for such an expansion, since we'll already have an unlimited supply of money. Similarly, record-keeping professionals such as bookkeepers and accountants will no longer be necessary, as there will be no "balance sheet" to produce. Once we decide to switch to an infinite economy, we'll all have to consider the impact of the change on our current careers, and to decide what other fields we would be interested in pursuing when the new economy is installed.

> "No man chooses evil because it is evil; he only mistakes it for happiness, for the good he seeks."
> - Mary Wollstonecraft (1759-1797)

HEALTH CARE

At this point it's almost impossible to think about health care without thinking about the monster it created: health insurance. Not long ago, becoming a doctor was considered a calling, like becoming a minister. Health care was priced for the people who used the services. It was simply expected that now and then a patient would be unable to afford the services, and this would be handled with payment plans or the occasional waiving of fees. As third-party payments became the norm, the prices reflected the financial capabilities of the corporation, not the patient. It then became impossible to afford basic health care without the sponsorship of the corporations. This means that parents who lack health insurance hesitate to have their children seen by doctors when problems develop, sick people are hustled out of hospitals or not seen at all because they can't produce an insurance card, and hordes of people live with a vague, chronic worry about what will happen if they should fall ill.

There have been two suggestions for how to resolve this crisis, both (naturally enough) within the system that made the crisis. The first is to work out a system that allows everybody to be insured. This solution will ensure that health care continues its trend toward ever more obscene pricing. The second is to eliminate insurance and make consumers feel the prices "with their pocketbooks," a solution designed to regulate costs by bringing them back into line with people's actual ability to pay. Since it's extremely unlikely that any doctor ten years into an expensive thirty-year mortgage will suddenly agree to charge a tenth of his present fees, it would appear that it's too late to make health care affordable. We pick at this problem in minor and almost completely ineffectual ways while it continues to accelerate far beyond our ability to ever grab a hold of it and resolve or at least control it.

In an infinite economy it just goes away. Everybody can afford health care because they have all the money they need. There will be no cynical money-grubbing among our physicians because they'll already have all the money they need, too. Our doctors will exist to treat our illnesses and to promote our good health. When we require their ministrations or their counsel, we will not need to hesitate to seek it.

EDUCATION

Our public schools are presently in dire straits, and the reason is lack of money. We have crowded classrooms, a poor supply of teaching materials, and - most importantly - insufficient funds to attract enough brilliant minds to the teaching profession. The teachers we have now are big-hearted enough to forego the possibility of wealth in order to do something they consider more important and valuable. Again, it's twisted to repay their valor

with a life of scraping along to make ends meet.
It's human nature to desire to pass on what we've learned from life. Our finite economy thwarts this very basic and generous impulse by making teaching an unaffordable professional choice. When all professional choices yield the same compensation of unlimited funds, we will almost certainly have a whole new force of people interested in teaching. We will additionally have school districts that are newly able to afford new classrooms or buildings and a wealth of educational materials. The result will be drastically improved student-teacher ratios, a new embrace of teaching as the quality contribution to society that it is, equal access to the most exciting, innovative, or proven teaching materials, and a drastic improvement in the entire system. There will no longer be "poor" districts across town from "rich" ones. Every family can afford to educate their children in the environment that seems best to them, and all environments will improve.

Every citizen who desires job training or a college education will be able to afford it. What's more, our institutions of higher learning can return to a focus on a rich and inspiring education rather than serving as a place to acquire credentials for employment. We all know a Liberal Arts major who couldn't find a job and works as a department store clerk, or a Languages major who switched to Engineering to be more marketable. The infinite economy allows - even encourages and demands - that everyone explore and develop their own genius out of their own impulses and inclinations. Rather than reduce our society to a conglomeration of people who must subvert their natures for the sake of getting a job, we will encourage our citizens to contribute their genius to society, with the belief that every human talent has value to humans.

WORKING CONDITIONS

At present many of our jobs, whether high-paying or at minimum subsistence level, have grueling working conditions. By the time people get ready for work, commute to the workplace, do the job, and get back home, they have little time to do something that they enjoy. If the job is particularly strenuous or depressing, they lack the energy as well. Most companies offer a grudging week or two of paid vacation after a minimum amount of uninterrupted working, usually a year. By the time the employee finally receives the vacation, the level of exhaustion often pre-empts enjoyment or refreshment. Our lives revolve around our work, work that many times is loathsome to us.

There is no reason for this, other than it's presently "how it's done" and we're used to it. We may fear that if productivity is low under a "40-hour week with two weeks vacation" system, it will truly deteriorate using a "30-hour week with six weeks vacation" system. Not so. Productivity isn't tied to how long and hard we work, it's tied to how smart we work. Many of our problems with productivity actually stem from the punishing system itself; the workers resent how little they get paid for how much of their lives they surrender to their jobs. They want to do as little as possible because their earnings don't reflect the effort they put into their jobs. Selling off one's life by the hour seems abhorrent, and a resistance to "giving their all" for their hourly wage seems a logical way to try to reclaim something for themselves. People know themselves to be far more valuable than any salary, and slacking off at work is nothing but an attempt to assert their value. If people didn't resist giving their all under our present system of compensation, it would say something pretty sad about our sense of ourselves as human beings. Is an hour of anyone's life really worth just $4.25, or even $10.00 or $100.00?

We've learned that a raise, even a substantial one, doesn't make us feel adequately compensated, and no finite amount ever will. An infinite economy compensates people with their true worth: infinity. The resentment that causes slacking off will disappear, and everyone's 30 hours will be far more productive than anyone's 40 or 50 or 60 hours ever was.

What's more, in an infinite economy everyone will perform work that interests them. The time we spend at work won't be the time we spend being dead inside. It will instead be the time we spend contributing our talents to our communities. Our current work environments lack both interesting, meaningful tasks and adequate compensation. Work environments in an infinite economy will provide us with both, so that we won't need to spend as much of our lives getting our jobs done. The infinite economy will encourage us to fill our time with quality things that we truly value, both on the job and at home.

"Man errs as long as he strives."
- Goethe (1749-1832)

BUSINESS FAILURE

The infinite economy operates on the honor system, in that everyone must find it within themselves to do their part and make a contribution to the system or see the system die. While the system encourages everybody to live their dream by supplying them with the means to do so, it also requires us to take a frank look at the response we're getting and to determine if we're contributing something of value. The feedback we receive for our endeavors will no longer be in the form of money, but in the form of needs filled and personal appreciation. If an individual starts something and finds few or no takers, they are asked - though not

forced - to move on to something else. We have to count on our respect for a worthwhile system to guide our decision making.
It's not impossible that we could have some cynical individuals who set up shop as, say, "insurance agent," find they have no takers, and continue to insist that they are an insurance agent who merely lacks business. This is unlikely, since everyone has talents and abilities that they like to show off and would welcome the chance to display what they've got, but we can't say it's impossible. If this should occur, we have to let it be, because it only reflects what a real human would be if given the chance to be anything he wanted to be.
What is more likely, though, is that the elimination of our financial constraints will give us the time and freedom to do more than we're currently doing. For every dullard who wants to take advantage of the system without giving anything back, we will have 500 people who happily contribute in more ways than their present means allow. Our desire to take advantage of the current system is strictly based on how poorly that system treats us, and not on something lazy and cynical in human nature. An infinite economy is likely to lift a cloud of disgust and despair from our hearts and to inspire a whole new desire to contribute all we have.
There is no clear-cut timetable for when we should feel compelled to declare our businesses a wash and move on; some things take more time to establish than others, and entrepreneurs can have all the time they need. What is crucial is that we gauge our usefulness as we go along, and if we have any doubt about our level of contribution, we augment our efforts with contributions in areas that we know to be necessary. Again, no one will force anyone to cooperate, but the system itself requires cooperation, and in order to implement it we need to commit to doing our share. Once more, this shouldn't be a burden because our share will have

meaning, be free of so many of our present unpleasantries, and earn unlimited compensation.

Throwing in the towel on a business endeavor will also be free of its current devastating effects, both financially and psychologically. The entire tone will be much more playful: you tried something, it didn't work out, you're on to something else. It was worth a shot. It will take us awhile to emerge from a system so full of needless junk and to create a system of quality in its stead, so that business failure will become the learning process it should be, and not the horrifying shake-up that it is.

UNEMPLOYMENT

In a word, there won't be any unemployment because we can't afford to have any. The infinite economy requires the talents of everyone willing and able to contribute. The vast majority of those people now unemployed want to work, and not just because they need to eat. A life spent doing nothing and stagnating isn't attractive to anyone; human beings incline to activity. It's frustrating to have talent and desire, and have no outlet for it. Our current system is a cynical one, in that it takes as its premise the idea that human nature must always be threatened with starvation and homelessness or it will fail to discover the motivation to do anything. When we were children we didn't have to be threatened with deprivation to make us build forts in the backyard, color in our coloring books, care for our baby dolls, or play "store." Just doing the adult version of those types of things will more or less answer all of our needs. We don't need threats to do them; we are human beings and there are things that human beings like to do. People who are unemployed experience both the deprivations and the frustrations that come from the inability to fulfill their own human impulses.

An infinite economy says that the threat is gone, and welcome aboard. To everyone.

"Can anybody remember when the times were not hard and money not scarce?"
- Ralph Waldo Emerson (1803-1882)

VOLUNTEERISM

As things stand, our work frequently exhausts and displeases us. It makes us bitter. Even if we have the emotional abilities to help others in their hour of need, we often lack the energy and the motivation. The demands of life suck us dry, and we have nothing to give to people who may need a hand. It takes a special person, under these conditions, to provide disaster relief, counsel the terminally ill, or teach the illiterate. The infinite economy, by encouraging meaningful work, providing us with unlimited means, and relieving us of the stress of the rat race, will enable us to come to the rescue of our fellows when trouble strikes.

In an infinite economy our livelihoods will be one aspect of our lives, not the centerpiece that requires all we've got that it presently is. We will have the freedom to design our lives and arrange our time according to our interests and abilities, in response to whatever needs become apparent in our communities. It would be hard to imagine a person who wouldn't get far more pleasure and satisfaction out of teaching an illiterate adult how to read, or rebuilding the local school that burned down, than they presently get out of hustling to sell some junk product to disinterested prospective buyers. Our system asks us to be weasely and try to "get over on people." The infinite economy asks us to discover our real needs and to fill them. A livelihood that doesn't leave you dead inside provides you with the energy and good-hearted motivation to do more with your free time than sit exhausted in front of your TV.

GENEROSITY AND PITY

Everyone has generous impulses. Unless our own frustrations and dissatisfactions have so embittered us that our focus has become frozen to our own neediness, we are saddened and moved by the sight of human suffering. We often do nothing beyond "feeling moved" because our system leaves us with so little to give. But even when we're able to follow through on our urge to render aid, our help is given in a spirit of pity that itself can be offensive. This is demonstrated by the fact that we have needy people who feel that their pride or self-respect would be violated if they "take charity." That's because our generosity often takes a tone that <u>does</u> violate self-respect and pride. The price of receiving aid, then, is too high for some, and for those who feel they are in no position to reject aid, they must acquiesce to the loss of pride that our form of giving generates.

This offensively pitying tone goes out the window in an infinite economy, because all citizens are automatically endowed with unlimited value, so that their sense of worth to society is never at stake. People don't like to be pitied; it's unpleasant. They want to be respected. It's no real consolation to anyone to know that their peers feel really, really sorry for them. Generous acts are tainted by the fact that massive pity is what currently motivates them.

The infinite economy can generate a whole new tenor to our generosity. Generosity won't mean spooning out the free lunch at the soup kitchen for the "poor souls" who can't afford their own food. Generosity will be the acts of worthwhile people coming to the aid of other worthwhile people who are experiencing problems of one sort or another. The problems won't be viewed as intractable the way they are now; they will be viewed as occasions to discover solutions.

Another form of generosity that the infinite economy will encourage is the sort that doesn't involve emergencies at all. This is the form of generosity that makes us want to surprise and delight the people we love. Many times we'll come across an item at a store that we know an aunt would love, but that we can't afford; or we take a vacation so wonderful that we'd love to go back with a friend, but we know it will never happen. Life is currently full of wonderful impulses that we have to quash. The infinite economy will allow us to act on those impulses without limit, providing us with the pleasure of giving wonderful things to the people we treasure.

> "The virtues of the poor may be readily admitted and are much to be regretted. We are often told that the poor are grateful for charity. Some of them are, no doubt, but the best amongst the poor are never grateful. They are ungrateful, discontented, disobedient, and rebellious. They are quite right to be so. Charity they feel to be a ridiculously inadequate mode of partial restitution, or a sentimental dole, usually accompanied by some impertinent attempt on the part of the sentimentalist to tyrannize over their private lives. Why should they be grateful for the crumbs that fall from the rich man's table? They should be seated at the board, and are beginning to know it."
> - Oscar Wilde (1854-1900)

THE INFINITE ECONOMY

NEUROSES

Before the advent of industrialized nations, neuroses were all but unheard of; in our culture they are everywhere. We are a people extremely ill at ease about many, many things. We look for the roots of our mental discomfort by doing things like sifting through our childhood memories to find something mean our parents said to us (as though parents were institutions and not people), or discovering how our high school boyfriend totally destroyed our ability to love. We're unhappy, and we need culprits. In an attempt to put ourselves at ease, we make bogeymen out of characters from our past, vilify them, "work through" the devastation they caused in our lives, and see if we feel any better. We usually do not.

The roots of our cultural discomfort probably have more to do with these types of things: most of us live our lives under an enormous amount of financial stress; it is hard to ever feel secure about money. The threat of destitution leads us to agree to spend huge chunks of our time doing boring, stupid stuff. Many of our jobs require us to essentially act as liars and cheats. Most of our jobs reward us for our efforts with a hand-to-mouth lifestyle. Essential services such as medical care are not at all guaranteed to us. We can't afford to raise our own children and end up having to leave them with people who don't love them like we do, so that we have to worry about what they're up to while we try to do a job we don't really like and wouldn't do if we had a choice.

These conditions don't just make us unhappy, they cripple us emotionally. We know that they do. Yet we pay our shrinks to tell us that we were never the same after our mother got mad, yelled "you fool!" and whacked us one, and that if we get in touch with that crucial traumatic event we can get better. We are willing to try this approach toward healing because our real malaise isn't something we can do very much about right now.

This is not to trivialize psychiatry, but the fact is that almost no one is actually cured by it. Nobody comes out of it whole, healed, happy, and joyously committed to life. That's because we use it to address the wrong things. It's probably true that people can learn something valuable about their past or about themselves through psychiatry. But they don't get better.

If we want to experience our lives as graceful and satisfying, then we need to create a graceful society that can satisfy. Nothing else - no field trip through the dark corners of our past, no self-indulgent contemplation of our attitudes toward sex - will do it. Improving one or another aspect of an essentially bruising economy will have an effect so minor as to be virtually imperceptible. We can only heal our broken spirits by allowing them to thrive in a healing society.

EXCUSES

When our lives fall short of our own expectations or the expectations of others, we often say "It's because I'm black/gay/poor/a woman/from the wrong side of town/from a broken family/disabled/Jewish/unable to afford the training" etc. etc. Certainly factors like these can interfere with realizing our goals, in that there is no doubting that certain sectors of our society are compelled to cope with economic disadvantage. The system of free market capitalism is designed to ensure that every member of society has a <u>chance</u> at economic betterment through hard work and determination. Theoretically, that is absolutely true. In reality, though, the discouragement level involved is hard to overcome when the disadvantage is extreme enough. The result is people living lives that don't satisfy them, armed with rationalizations that may be true enough, but that don't improve anything and only succeed in adding a bitter twist to failure.

The infinite economy will bring a welcome end to our rationalizations and excuse-making. We will all be armed with the means to realize our goals, so that any failings will be our own responsibility. The rationalization process renders us essentially adolescent, unable to face up to our own limitations and attempt to correct them; we have too large and often valid an opportunity to pass the buck.

Human beings are diverse; our diversity is what makes us capable of making a rich society viable. This means that we have a broad spectrum of talents and intelligences, and an infinite economy will recognize and welcome this. This does mean, though, that failure is perfectly possible: you just may not "have the stuff" to do what you thought you could. But the failings will be your own, not the result of the economic oppressions of your particular group. If you try to be something and find that you can't pull it off, you can't say that you weren't it because of the economic hardship you were dealt. If you weren't it, it's because you really <u>weren't</u> it.

Some of the excuses we hear today break our hearts. Some of them just make us roll our eyeballs. The infinite economy will bring an end to both, so that we're all called upon to make our tries and take our lumps as the responsible adults we have to be.

CRIMINALITY

To the extent that crime is motivated by money, crime will no longer exist. That extent is quite obviously large. It's true that there are "crimes of passion" motivated by jealousy, and there are rapes and drunken drivers and other assorted anti-social, violent, or criminal acts that an infinite economy will fail to resolve. But most crime will disappear under such a system, as the motivation for it will be completely removed.

Far from being "nuts," our criminals act in ways completely rational on an individual, if not social, level. There is no mysterious evil force animating their hearts. Without idealizing criminals as "victims of society," it can't be disputed that almost all criminals are desperate people frustrated by an unfriendly and punitive system of economics. A society so unjust and trying for so many of its members is bound to inspire anti-social acts. We only need to consider the over-crowded state of our jails and the fact that crime, rather than diminishing, continues to surge to know that our social approach is simply not effective. It might be different if our prisons were places where frustrated people were taught to unleash their genius and become millionaires - in other words, places where people could actually learn how to maneuver successfully in our economic system - but they're not. We take individuals so desperate and hopeless that they are inspired to criminality, make them sit out for awhile, and return them to the very system that caused their original desperation. We pretty much know that criminals are people crippled by our system, and that we ought to have compassion for them, but compassion is the first thing to go out the window when we're the victims of criminal acts. We want them in jail where they can do no more harm, but where they also have no opportunity to heal or to improve. We thus have a vicious cycle and no meaningful way to shatter it.

This is an area that is absolutely irreparable under our present system of economics. It cannot get better using solutions available in a finite economy: for every criminal marginally rehabilitated in a prison program we have dozens more just beginning to reach their boiling point and preparing to lash out. We seem to want disadvantaged people to find a way to come to peace with their difficult place in life, and this is too much to ask.

Like all people, criminals are attempting to assert their sense of value and deservingness in a system that tells them they have none. If we lack the means to elicit contributions from people and value them for it, we will have criminals.

Rather than operating from a base of presumed rejection that must be battled and overcome, an infinite economy invites and welcomes - even demands - the contributions of its participants, and values those contributions. Our presence as citizens of our society endows us with unlimited value, and our society awaits our contribution. In this way an infinite economy not only eliminates money as a motive for crime, it also relieves us of the frustrating psychological components that inspire anti-social behavior. It heals both sides of the criminal equation.

The infinite economy also addresses the criminal inspiration among our wealthy members of society, in that the insecurity of standing atop a house of cards will be eliminated. Wealth won't run out, because there is no end to it and that's that, and we can think about other things now. What's more, the finite economy has a tendency to reward wealth in and of itself with more wealth, and this can make our wealthy citizens psychologically uneasy. They are never asked to contribute anything, since wealth exempts us from work in our finite system. The infinite economy asks for the genius of all its members, generating the possibility of well-rounded human endeavors and satisfactions for everyone.

The finite system, while obviously "neutral" in that it intends no ill will to its participants, often generates the sensation that it is actually hateful, rejecting, and unwelcoming. Criminals are people who respond to that sensed hatred by hating the system right back, in the form of anti-social acts. A system that generates so much hate should clearly be re-thought. An infinite system of welcome and reward takes the hate factor out of society and transforms its participants into secure people who are eager to cooperate.

An infinite economy will also cause some areas of illegality to be cast in an entirely different light. For example, prostitution is now illegal in almost all of America. It appears a crime of exploitation, something that no woman would want to do if her economic circumstances were not desperate. It appears that men take advantage of female economic vulnerability in a shatteringly personal manner. In an infinite economy prostitution will face the same test that all livelihoods will confront: would millionaires do it? The exploitation i.e. criminal factor will be removed, and we will be left with nothing but genuinely human impulses. If we have infinitely wealthy people who want to run fantasy brothels, and we have financially independent women who are willing to work in them, and we have willing clientele, then we will have prostitution. If any of the elements prove non-existent, prostitution will just die out. We have to be open to whatever it is that truly free human beings are moved to do and be, so that we can find out what it is that we contain.

The same will be true for the illegal drug trade. Peasants grow crops that will earn them the most money because they are desperately poor and need to act in accord with their own needs for survival. If they were free of that struggle, would they still want to cultivate cocaine-producing crops? If they did, would we have infinitely wealthy people who felt their calling was to refine and distribute it? Would a population suddenly given the means to realize their wildest dream in actuality still be interested in the "fake joy" that cocaine momentarily provides? If all of these things are freely chosen, then we will continue to have drug use in accord with people's actual desire for it. If anything is missing in the equation, drugs will become a rarity or be non-existent in our society.

THE INFINITE ECONOMY

Addiction itself, though certainly possessed of physiological elements, is just as certainly a result of a society that thwarts our hopes, dreams, and best ambitions. Experiencing the effects of drugs or alcohol is superior to experiencing reality. When we create a society that supports our aspirations and allows us to actualize our goals and experience our best selves, a make-believe moment of euphoria will pale in comparison. Right now many people think "Why should I struggle and suffer when I can generate a euphoric state with this substance?" In an infinite system people may well ask "Why settle for groundless euphoria when I can get the real thing by realizing my best dreams?"

There will no doubt be people who will continue to enjoy their glass of wine with dinner, their six-pack while they watch a ballgame, their weekend joint with friends, or their snort of cocaine at a party. But these people are not and never were "the drug problem," in that this type of "I-just-want-to-put-my-feet-up-and-relax-and-have-a-good-time" mentality has never been a threat to a successful social system. The threat exists when large numbers of our population drop out of social participation in order to provide themselves with some measure of emotional satisfaction. If we can create a society that provides satisfactions of all kinds for its members, we won't have people who need to exit it in order to experience some pleasure in a world of bitter disappointment.

"Starvation, and not sin, is the parent of modern crime."
- Oscar Wilde (1854-1900)

"Where justice is denied, where poverty is enforced, where ignorance prevails, and where any one class is made to feel that society is in an organized conspiracy to oppress, rob,

and degrade them, neither persons nor property will be safe."
- Frederick Douglass (c.1818-1895)

"The same energy of character which renders a man a daring villain would have rendered him useful to society, had that society been well organized."
- Mary Wollstonecraft (1759-1797)

"The lack of money is the root of all evil."
- Mark Twain (1835-1910)

CORPORATE GREED

We can't trust our corporations because they exist to make money and will do anything to achieve that goal. They will lie about their products until the government makes them stop. They will encourage unethical behavior in the name of keeping the corporate entity afloat. They will unleash a sales force trained to put maximum pressure on potential buyers, even to the degree of holding "sales training sessions" designed to teach the sales force how to manipulate their leads psychologically. They will only turn their attention to "quality" if it's affordable; if not, corporations have no problem trying to pass off shoddy products and will not stop doing so until the law intervenes. Even when the law intervenes, there are usually years and years of expensive litigation during which the corporation continues to push its product. Corporations pollute our air and water because they "can't afford" to be concerned with the environment: it would cut too deeply into profits.

The rationalization that allows these unappealing factors to continue and to even be considered necessary is that corporations support our families. If we didn't have corporations generating wealth and concerned with the "bottom line," we would put all of those workers and their families into impoverishment. Corporate greed is a necessary evil in a finite economy. We work for large corporations and use our money to buy their products.

Large corporations will probably exist in an infinite economy, but the entire dynamic of priorities will change dramatically. Every corporation will be able to afford - and will have an obligation to consider - the environmental impact of its operation. Each organization can hire an environmental team to improve its operations and possibly to suggest new ways of clean manufacturing that we haven't been able to "afford" dreaming of yet. Can we send all of our waste in rocket to the sun instead of burying it in the earth? Could anything hurt the sun? An infinite economy will give us the means to ask any question about environmental issues, allow us to look into possible solutions in every conceivable way, and then allow us the means to execute the solutions the instant they are developed.

Another major focus of every corporation will be the quality of its products, and there will be ample money to improve those products in every way. High-pressure sales people will not be necessary when products of sterling quality are being offered and the necessity of making sales through any and all means is removed. Corporations that exploit their workers will find themselves without employees. In an infinite economy the corporate "bottom line" will not be the balance sheet, but rather the ability to attract and hold willing contributors. The value center will be shifted from money to people. If a corporation wants to remain afloat, it must offer exciting and useful quality products and invent corporate structures that satisfy all the participants. If nobody really wants to work on an assembly line, those type of corporate environments will disappear, replaced by custom-made items of quality generated and sold in our own communities. Any corporation in an infinite economy will simply be a group of people united to produce something that couldn't be produced otherwise, all of whom will agree about the value of what they're working to realize. As always, employees unwilling to cooperate with the corporate vision will find themselves in need of a new livelihood. By the same token, corporations unwilling to cooperate with the employee vision will find themselves in need of new employees. A corporation so insensitive that it doesn't deserve employees just won't have them.

LAW

The world is large, opinions are diverse, and different countries, states and cities will have varying ideas about what should and should not be legal. As is presently the case, different populations will have the right to develop laws as they see fit in an infinite economy. As has been demonstrated, many of the crimes that burden our legal system will just cease to be in an infinite economy. There will just as obviously be plenty of others that humanity will still have to cope with and attempt to resolve.

What we won't have is money-motivated lawyers encouraging us to seek financial compensation every time something bad happens to us. We won't have corporations that knowingly sell us injurious products in order to get their hands on our money, so that product flaws will actually be "honest mistakes," and remedies immediately undertaken. We won't have "breach of contract" suits that drag on for years, enrich the legal profession, and do nothing to foster quality in our lives: if contracts are broken, it will only mean that one party lost interest in an endeavor, there are no financial implications, and the remaining party is free to seek another party interested in the endeavor. The legal profession is motivated by "billable hours" and the prospect of big cash settlements to far too great a degree. Money is not what law should be about. It reduces our attempts at social justice to the exchange of dollar bills. A legal system should concern itself with the rights and responsibilities of its citizens. Human beings have a lot of questions to ask about this. Our present system prevents us from getting to the meat of what law is all about because it encourages us to use the legal system to get money in return for perceived injustices. Our attention is fixed on the legal system as a means of extracting some value for ourselves, and not about true law.

It should be within the capacity of human beings to develop legal systems that define rights and clarify responsibilities. Too much of our mode of justice administration is tied up in "it's not fair - give me some money." This is too frequently nothing but the whininess of people unwilling to take responsibility for the outcome of their decisions, and who see a golden opportunity to obtain money in a world where golden opportunities seldom present. The system is cynical and immature, and only encourages cynicism and immaturity. We need instead to address what constitutes an actual injustice and to determine effective methods to correct it. Surrendering money will no longer be punitive, obviously, or even meaningful. We will need to consider loss of freedom, or of particular rights, or certain services to the community, or loss of accredation as the vehicles of justice. But all questions of justice will be about justice and not about money changing hands.

GOVERNMENTS

Governments are necessary to define the social contract (i.e. laws) and to oversee projects that benefit the population, such as space programs, the care of national parks, the preservation of historical documents and artifacts, health programs, and so on. Populations should be free to select their method of government and to staff it with people who will act in the best interests of that population.

This is theoretically what we have right now, but we know that there is nothing more corrupt than government in a finite economy. We don't have representatives who will act in our best interests, we have representatives who will act in the best interests of the guy with the biggest bribe. We have candidates who win elections based on how much money they had available to buy TV time. We have lobbyists sent specifically to protect the polluting rights of the corporations that pay them. We have politicians who base their entire campaigns on the proper uses of the "taxpayer's money," and not about solutions to real social problems.

In an infinite economy all manner of political corruption will vanish. It will be impossible to buy anybody's vote. Our representatives will be people who feel called to represent us, and they will have to explain why and be convincing. We will actually be able to trust our politicians - something nearly unthinkable now.

An infinite system will also eliminate heaps of bureaucracy. There will be no income taxes, for example, since the government will have all the funds it needs, too. It won't have to skimp on worthwhile projects, and none of its infinitely paid employees will be caught with their hand in the cookie jar. Governments can run smoothly and efficiently if they are peopled by sincere representatives and if money is no object. An infinite economy will cause both of these conditions to be actualized.

Bureaucracy is the result of attempts to patch up the problems of a flawed system. As flaws appear in our governmental systems, bureaucratic solutions arise in an attempt to keep the system above water. We need only to look at the convoluted heaps of governmental bureaucracy to know how many flaws our system is attempting to hide. We need to institute an efficient system of government, one that allows us to ditch the bureaucratic tangle completely and re-focus our governmental institutions on their proper functions. An infinite economy will allow us to do that.

"There are a thousand hacking at the branches of evil to one who is striking the root."
- Henry David Thoreau (1817-1862)

THE MILITARY

The state of Pennsylvania never raised a special army to defend its border with Ohio. No Pennsylvanian ever lost sleep worrying that Ohio was preparing an invasion. All 50 American states know themselves to be completely secure divisions of one larger entity. If you live in a state that doesn't produce lumber or automobiles, you just buy some from a state that does. You never consider attacking Detroit and seizing the automobile plants for the state of Nevada - it makes no sense at all. No one would ever want to use military might to obtain things when the simple exchange of money would yield the identical result with no death or destruction.

In this way the 50 states are a model of what the world can be, a model of almost indifferent cooperation. We can perceive the countries of the world as secure divisions of a larger entity, the world. With our common currency we can freely exchange whatever it is we have. If Japan really does make the best cars, and if nobody thinks of a better way to make them, then we'll get our cars from Japan. It will be no different than a Texan buying a Detroit-made car.

It should be clear that such an understanding will create an environment where war, and thus the military as it presently exists, will be unnecessary. We will consider ourselves one unit divided into sections of rich and spectacular diversity. However, the history of humanity so far has mostly been the history of war, and it will take us awhile to get used to this. While we get our infinite economy underway, the nations that maintain armies should continue to do so while we make the adjustment and become secure in the system.

Serving one's country has always been a good and inspiring idea. It's just that, with little exception, such service has meant standing ready to kill enemies of the country. As the new system takes hold, the purpose of the organized military will evolve as well. It should be useful for governments to maintain the type of training and experience the military presently provides for its participants, but its purpose can change. "The Service" can be groups of people who stand ready to be called to areas of natural disaster, to completely re-do and beautify communities that exist in ghetto conditions, to repair roads and bridges, and so on. They can actually serve their populations by improving lives, and this type of service will have much more meaning and direct impact than standing ready to kill enemies.

The military has fulfilled its historical directive and done it brilliantly. But organizing citizens to kill people in order to prove points should be as alien to our global community as it is to our 50 states. We have far better things to do with our talents.

IMMIGRATION

An infinite economy with a common global currency will truly unite the world. We won't need passports or visas or green cards or alien registrations or what have you in order to live and work where we desire. Governments won't have to close their doors to immigrants, because there will be no financial burden associated with immigration. People will be able to settle where they like, in the same way that Americans move from state to state with complete freedom and no bureaucratic processing or hold up.

In order to make a successful adjustment to this new freedom, we should all attempt to assimilate our new wealth right where we are. We should apply our talents and our wealth to improving the communities that gave us birth. We should give our present locations a shot at fulfilling our dreams. Then we can gradually readjust so that world citizens can gravitate to the locales that most appeal to them.

Most of the motivation for a desire to relocate is about poverty and lack of opportunity. The infinite economy will eliminate poverty and generate an abundance of new opportunities, and it will do this everywhere. Immigration will be about the desire to live under certain attractive governments, or about the desire to live in a place one finds beautiful and inspiring. The end result will be people living in environments that satisfy them.

REAL ESTATE

We know that people want to be secure about their own homes and that government ownership and distribution of land is probably not a very workable idea. We will continue to need vehicles like deeds that bestow property rights in order to avoid chaotic situations. The challenge will be in the adjustment period while we settle into the reality of our infinite economy.

In a way similar to how we'll need to adjust to our employment situations and our immigration impulses, when we begin we should all sit tight for the moment and work from where we are. One of the first uses of our new wealth should be applied to making our present homes into our dream homes. If they then fail to satisfy us for whatever reasons, we should begin the process of undertaking a move.

If we first turn our attention to beautifying our homes, there will be no more "bad side of town." Many of our urban ghettos have deteriorated to their horrendous conditions because the occupants have been unable to afford improvements, or even basic care. In the infinite economy these same people will have the means to actualize their desire for a graceful neighborhood. Apartments will be painted, new bathrooms put in, flower boxes will appear in windows. Buildings that are structurally unsound can be razed and rebuilt. We can spend as much time - and money - as we want to on the improvements. Every existing dwelling can be transformed into a first-class one, and new housing developments can incorporate the best of everything, and easily find occupants. As we gradually make these improvements and transformations, real estate transactions can be handled through the means that currently exist. Your real estate agent will be someone who loves matching people to their dream homes, and there will be no pressure on that agent to make the commission. You can be secure about having your true interests served.

Our homes will also be places that reflect our aesthetic interests and conform to our desires. In other words, we will buy homes to live in, not to speculate on and try to "make a killing" on a few years down the road. Homes will be places to raise our families, to throw our parties, to house our out-of-town friends.

There will be no motive for any individual to horde housing; "landlord" will not be a livelihood, although "building superintendent" and "real estate agent" will be. The obscenity of real estate speculation will end, and housing will be available to everyone. No one will have to settle for anything less than a cozy dwelling that meets their own ideas about what a home should be.

PRIMITIVE SOCIETIES

The infinite economy is the necessary solution to the problems of "modern" civilization. Modern folks may pine for a return to simpler ways, in the belief that if we went back to the old ways the problems that weren't yet apparent in our system would once again become invisible. Our modern system, however, can't be erased. We can't pretend that we didn't learn, grow, and change irrevocably through our participation in the historical events of this century. We have become something new. Going backwards is not an option for us. We have to develop new solutions to the problems of modernity and act upon those solutions from where we really are. It won't help us to imagine that people will surrender the fruits of progress in order to eliminate homelessness or solve the health care crisis. An infinite economy can take away many of our problems and keep us moving forward and growing.

There are, of course, societies that have not participated in the surge of modernity, societies that have developed completely satisfying methods of community life who have no need for this solution. The beauty of the infinite economy is that it offers the means for anyone with interest to fully participate in it without forcing anyone to change anything about their way of life if they don't want to. The infinite economy protects primitive societies by making their exploitation impossible. Every citizen of the known world will have complete access to the global currency any time they want it. No society may be enslaved or exploited.

Primitive societies that have survived into the modern age have served to carry the torch of graceful living for the rest of us. Their methods of operating a social system are often beautiful and inspiring. These societies may well wish to continue their brilliant counterpoint to modern life. Without the hardships that invasion and enslavement have brought to these cultures, they will be free to create their societies in peace.

They will also find themselves warmly welcomed in the event they have any interest in participating in any aspect of modern life.

SPIRITUAL SEARCH

It has often been expressed that money poisons one spiritually. The worship of money, or even an intense focus on it, can certainly cripple us in terms of the other more profound, richer, and often more satisfying and meaningful aspects of existence. If all we can think about is money, we aren't able to turn to the basic questions of humanity's relation to itself and to divinity. We become pathetically superficial and one-dimensional.

Yet in a system of finite economics, who <u>doesn't</u> focus on money? We have to, or we won't eat. From the wealthiest members or our society to the poorest, we are all asked to constantly consider how we can best get money to come our way. Fretting over how we're ever going to pay the rent is not a spiritual exercise. Feeling frustrated and panicked because the local plant is closing and our jobs are gone is not a spiritual exercise. Having to work two jobs in order to meet the bills only manages to eat up our time and attention and leaves us with little opportunity to ask the kind of questions that could enrich our lives.

THE INFINITE ECONOMY 63

In order to fulfill ourselves spiritually we have to stop our focus on money. The answer is not to be poor and have no money; the answer is to have access to all the money we need so that we don't have to clog our thoughts with plotting to get some. Only when we're secure about money can we turn our attention to better things. We don't know the properties of the divine mind, we don't know how men and women can best love each other, we don't know how to overcome jealousy, we don't know how we can best educate our children. But we do know how to manufacture money; it is something that human beings can easily do. As long as we refuse to crack the whole thing wide open and pass money around freely, we're all doomed to dwell on it obsessively. Once we do it, we can finally be free to consider the other more profound questions about our existence.

There is a catch-phrase in the New Age movement that goes: "It's an abundant universe." Well, it is, but not because there is money or gold or diamonds hidden in it that we can extract through the power of our thoughts. The universe is abundant because it will allow us to value anything we want to, thereby leaving it in our own hands to design our level of wealth. The universe didn't decide what was valuable, we did. We created a harsh and trying system out of our beliefs about what had value and what didn't. We're free to change that anytime we want to. In fact, we *have* changed it many times as the system evolved through time. The universe will never refuse us if we want to dramatically increase the value pool.

Another catch phrase of the New Age movement is "You create your own reality." We have people who want to take responsibility for whatever happens to them and who seek to improve their lives through their own efforts. Common methods for doing this include meditation, chanting, visualization, examining one's beliefs, developing one's faith in a benevolent creator, changing one's associations, and so forth. But why should it be so hard to create our own reality? Why should it take massive effort and what amounts to self-hypnosis to get the universe to budge so much as one inch? Why shouldn't it be easy for human beings to live the way that human beings like to live? We should all have jobs we like and homes that reflect our tastes. We should all be free to go see the wonders of this world and enjoy and appreciate them. We should all spend time with the people that we love. And we shouldn't have to push with all our might to make those things happen. A system that thwarts almost everybody's dreams is not a system worth keeping. We need a system that can support our most gorgeous dreams almost as fast as we can think them up. The only thing that stops us, over and over again, is not God but our economic conditions. It is in our power to take that hurdle away and begin to discover our own capabilities.

Mankind may or may not be the handiwork of a divine mind. So far mankind isn't even the handiwork of mankind, in that we haven't set up a system that will allow us to create ourselves out of whatever it is we've got. An infinite economy can free us to be what we really are. Once we know what that is, we may be able to comprehend how it relates to the universe at large.

> "Money, it turned out, was exactly like sex: you thought of nothing else if you didn't have it and thought of other things if you did."
> - James Baldwin (1924-1987)

> "It is too difficult to think nobly when one only thinks to get a living."
> - Jean Jacques Rousseau (1712-1778)

GENIUS

Money can't and never will buy genius. You can't pay a guy and get him to compose like Mozart or write like Shakespeare. Unending streams of money won't miraculously cause us to produce enduring masterpieces en masse. But it sure will invite us to do so. It sure will ask us to think about the best things we have within us and leave us free to express it. We have no way of knowing how much buried genius went to the grave with our slaves, or with people forced to spend their lives struggling just to get by. We'll never recover what we've lost, but we can make sure we never lose anything again.

We frequently bemoan the fact that history has apparently taught us nothing about how people should live: we still have wars, prejudice, cruelty, poverty, jealousy, exploitation, and millions of people dying frustrated and sad. It often appears that humanity exists only to repeat the same horrifying cycle of struggle and privation. This makes us feel worthless and causes our suffering to appear meaningless. If this is true, let's learn something now. Let's shatter the cycle and endow our lives with value and meaning. The solution is simple and elegant and couldn't be easier to institute. We can discover what kind of geniuses we are individually, and we can make humanity the masterpiece that it can and should be.

There's nothing that says we have to do it. But there's nothing to stop us, either.

"Never yet has law formed a great man: 'tis liberty that breeds giants and heroes."
- J.C.F. von Schiller (1759-1805)

TRANSACTIONS

Human beings are physical entities and material things matter to us. There are some things we couldn't understand without physical demonstrations using concrete materials. This is why it is imperative that we begin our infinite economy by minting actual currency, passing it around, and using it for our value transactions. It will help us to understand what we're doing. Real money will allow us to get used to an infinite system.

Historically we know that if we introduce more money into a system, prices rise accordingly and we end up not much different from where we started. The only way to bust out of the cycle is to introduce infinity to the system. No house will cost "infinity," nor will any of the other necessities of life. Using infinity changes the entire mathematical structure of economics. Our material needs are always finite. An infinite economy is the only way to ensure that the management of those finite needs will be under our control.

It may take us any number of years to develop a society using infinite means, and the use of currency will get us through that adjustment. Once we get the hang of what infinity means, we can switch to plastic cards. From there it will be no time before we run our society on no transactions at all. Flash a card that we know everyone has three or four times, and we won't really need to do it after that. We will have a society that values every citizen within it, and citizens making contributions to it guided by their best inner light.

DOES THE WHOLE WORLD HAVE TO AGREE TO AN INFINITE ECONOMY FOR IT TO WORK?

It would certainly make world relations more positive and an adjustment to an infinite economy simpler if everyone agreed to start it at the same time. The benefits of an infinite economy are so obvious that it shouldn't be impossible to have such an agreement among nations. Failing that, however, it would not be impossible for a nation to act as a "laboratory" for the system so that anyone nervous about it could witness the outcome.

A country with severe economic problems, such as the former Soviet Union, might feel that there was nothing to lose by trying such a system, and the other nations of the world should respect the experiment if it is undertaken. It would be useful to begin by compensating the present citizens with unlimited funds and soliciting their best talents. An "S.O.S. Newsletter" should go out to the citizens of other countries listing areas of need, perhaps for skills in home building, medicine, agriculture, corporate development, or what have you. Anyone interested in giving their all for unlimited compensation could join the experiment, regardless of national origin. Other countries interested in recognizing the infinite currency could join the system. If people enjoy living under an infinite system, all the nations of the world could eventually join it.

It would probably be preferable if we could reach agreement before we began; that way we would have access to the talents of every individual in order to make a go of it. If that kind of consensus proves impossible, however, the system should still be tried and assessed. The end result should be the same, whichever way we choose to go about it.

WHAT AN INFINITE ECONOMY WON'T DO

An infinite economy can solve a great deal of our problems. But it won't solve them all. An infinite system won't relieve us of our racial prejudice, our religious intolerance, our jealousy, the inequality of our various talents. It won't tell us how best to confront whatever antisocial behavior we have left. It won't explain how best to govern ourselves. It won't tell us how to parent our children, or how many bad words are acceptable during prime time. It won't provide us with the blueprint for the sanest use of our natural resources. It won't cure cancer or AIDS. It won't teach us how to worship God, or resolve the abortion debate.

Most of the things that an infinite economy won't address can be beautifully resolved with one sweeping cure: love. Once we ditch our economic problems, we can get busy figuring out that one.

Q.E.D.

For money has a power above
The stars and fate, to manage love.
- Samuel Butler (1835-1902)

And only the Master shall praise us, and only the Master shall blame;
And no one shall work for money, and no one shall work for fame,
But each for the joy of working, and each, in his separate star,
Shall draw the Thing as he sees It for the God of Things as They are!
- Rudyard Kipling (1865-1936)

If I were asked to state the great objective which Church and State are both demanding for the sake of every man and woman and child in this country, I would say that that great objective is "a more abundant life."
- Franklin D. Roosevelt (1882-1945)

I wish that every human life might be pure transparent freedom.
- Simone de Beauvoir (1908-1986)

Some men see things as they are and say, "Why?" I dream things that never were and say, "Why not?"
- Robert F. Kennedy (1925-1968)

INDEX OF INSPIRATION:

Adams, Abigail
Adams, John
Aristotle
B-52s
Baldwin, James
Barry, Dave
Beardsley, Aubrey
Beatles
Beethoven
Behn, Aphra
Bell, Daniel
Bierce, Ambrose
Bill and Ted
Blake, William
Blanc, Mel
Boethius
Boorstin, Daniel
Bowie, David
Branaugh, Kenneth
Brooks, Albert
Brown, A. Whitney
Buddha
Burton, Richard

Campbell, Joseph
Cantor, George
Carse, James
Chartier, Emile
Cipriano, Rosemarie & Ralph
Clark, Kenneth
Cole, Peter
Cornyetz, Danny
Cousins Family
Cuomo, Mario

de Beauvoir, Simone
de Tocqueville, Alexis
Disney, Walt
Dolby, Thomas
Douglass, Frederick

Elfman, Danny
Emerson, Ralph Waldo
Emmanuel
Euclid

Flickinger, Ed
Frank, Anne
Franken, Al
Franklin, Benjamin
Fuhrer, Chelsea

Gabriel, Peter
Gallegos, Eddie and Deonna
Gawain, Shakti
Goethe, Johann
Goldman, Emma
Goldman, Steve
Grateful Dead
Groening, Matt
Grof, Stanislav
The Guide
Guthrie, Michael

Hardy, G.H.
Hegel, G.W.F.
Hellman, Lillian
Howarth, Jamie
Hughes, Robert

Ife, Leah and John
Ingersoll, Robert

Jackson, Art
Jackson, Jesse
Jeffers, Robinson
Jefferson, Thomas
Jesus
Jesus Jones
Jones, Chuck
Jung, Carl

Kaelin Family
Kandinsky, Wassily
Keillor, Garrison
Kennedy, Robert
Kennedy, John F.
Kepler
Keyes, Ken
Keynes, John Maynard
King, Martin Luther
King, Coretta Scott

Lincoln, Abraham
Lubarsky Group

Marx, Karl
Mead, Margaret
Melville, Herman
Mercouris, Joylyn
Michael, George
Michelangelo
Moyers, Bill
MST 3K
Mulligan, Chris
Murray, Patti

Nehru, Jawaharlal
Nietzche, Friedrich
NYC

Oetjen, Curtis and Cherie
Oppenheimer, J. Robert
Overn, Michael

Parrish, Maxfield
Pepys, Samuel
Pericles
Pico, Giovanni
Plato
Prince
Ptahhotpe
Publilius Syrus

Ramanajan
Rand, Ayn
Reece Graphics
Rice, Anne
Robbins, Tony
Roberts, Jane
Roberts, Steve and Patty
Rodegast, Pat
Roosevelt, Franklin D.
Rottenberg, Dan
Rousseau, Jean Jacques
Rudnick, Paul

Schumpeter, Joseph
Science, Dr.
Seth
Shakespeare, William
Smith, Matt & Sherry
Solon

Steely Dan
Steinem, Gloria
Stern, Howard
Stevens, Wallace
Sting

Talking Heads
Tarnas, Richard
Tawney, Richard Henry
Thompson, Emma
Thoreau, Henry David
Torso, Greg
Tovsky, Bruce
Toynbee, Arnold
Treffinger, Gary
Trilling, Lionel
Tucker, Sophie
Turner, Ted
Twain, Mark

U2

Van Buren, Abigail
Velhagen, Eric
Venus
Voltaire
von Schiller, J.C.F.
Von Neumann, John
Vulinovic, Kim and Dan

Walberg, Harry
Walker, Jay
Warren, Janet
Was (Not Was)
Waters, John
Weil, Simone
Whitman, Walt
Wilde, Oscar
Williamson, Marianne
Wolff, Bobby
Wolfe, Thomas
Wollstonecraft, Mary
World Party
World Series

XTC

Yeltsin, Boris

Zappa, Frank